The Super3®

INFORMATION SKILLS
FOR YOUNG LEARNERS

Michael B. Eisenberg and
Laura Eisenberg Robinson

Linworth Books

**Professional Development Resources for
K-12 Library Media and Technology Specialists**

Library of Congress Cataloging-in-Publication Data

Eisenberg, Michael.

  The Super3: Information Skills for Young Learners / Michael B. Eisenberg and Laura Eisenberg Robinson.
    p. cm.
  Includes index.
  ISBN 1-58683-286-7 (pbk.)
  1. Information retrieval--Study and teaching (Elementary). 2. Information retrieval--Study and teaching
(Elementary)--United States. 3. Electronic information resource literacy--Study and teaching (Elementary)
4. Electronic information resource literacy--Study and teaching (Elementary)--United States. I. Robinson,
Laura I. II. Title.
  ZA3075.E415 2007
  025.04'0712--dc22
                              2007010592

Cynthia Anderson: Acquisitions Editor
Carol Simpson: Editorial Director
Judi Repman: Consulting Editor

Published by Linworth Publishing, Inc.
3650 Olentangy River Road, Suite 250
Worthington, Ohio 43214

ISBN: 1-58683-286-7

5 4 3 2 1

Table of Contents

Table of Figures

Dedications

To My "Super3": Anthony, Logan, and Leah with a "shout out" to Uncle.
LR

And to Everyone's #1 – wife, mom, and grandma Carol, of course!
ME

About the Authors

Mike Eisenberg is Dean Emeritus and Professor at the Information School of the University of Washington. He stepped down as dean in 2006 after transforming that school into a powerhouse. For many years, Mike worked as Professor of information studies at Syracuse University and as founding Director of the Information Institute of Syracuse (including the ERIC Clearinghouse on Information & Technology, AskERIC, and GEM, the Gateway to Education Materials). Mike and Bob Berkowitz created the Big6 approach to information literacy, and he has worked with thousands of students— pre-K through higher education—as well as people in business, government, and communities to improve their information and technology skills. Mike's current work focuses on information, communications, and technology (ICT) literacy, information credibility, and information science education K-20.

Laura Eisenberg Robinson is a special education teacher within the Seattle School District. Laura recently started her 6th year with the Seattle Schools and currently works with Kindergarten through fifth grade students. Previously to working in Seattle, Laura taught in upstate New York for 5 years. In addition to teaching, Laura is an editor and project manager for Big6 Associates. She incorporates the Big6 and Super3 into her teaching on a daily basis. Most recently, Laura edited *The Big6 Collection: The Best of the Big6 eNewsletter, Volume II*, with her father, Mike Eisenberg. Laura feels very fortunate to be able to collaborate and work with her Dad.

Chapter 1

INTRODUCTION: THE SUPER3™

THE PURPOSE OF THE SUPER3: LEARNING AND MASTERING PROCESS

Welcome to the Super3!

This is an upbeat, positive, can-do book. It's about how educators, parents, and care-givers can help young students to succeed at whatever they want to do. Young students can learn to become much better thinkers and problem-solvers by learning and focusing on "process." But, it's not easy to do this—to explain to young children about process.

That's where the Super3 comes in, because at its core, that's what the Super3 is—a process. We want young students to be super at Super3 BEGINNING: Plan, MIDDLE: Do, END Review; to be better at "process."

Process is:

- a way of doing things.
- a course of action.
- a plan.
- an approach.
- a method.

The Super3 is all about "process." It's a "process model" with 3 parts that is simple and helpful. The Super3 does not force children into doing things a certain way. Rather, the Super3 provides a framework for students to learn how to get things done.

Yes, we encourage students to start the process with Part 1 and then move on to Part 2 and Part 3, but if they do not follow the specific order, that's okay! They can always come back to Part 1 later or branch out or jump around. The Super3 isn't narrow or restrictive. It is flexible because people are flexible.

BUT, from our experience, we find that overall success in a task or assignment does require success in each of the Super3 parts. While it is fine to jump around or start in the middle, it is important to be able to do each of the 3 parts.

So, the purpose of the Super3 is to provide a "process" for children to learn and use in order to be successful in whatever task they undertake. Teachers, families, and care-givers can help students to be successful by teaching them how to use the Super3.

FIRST LOOK: THREE SUPER PARTS

The Super3 follows the familiar narrative style of a story. Most stories have three parts: a beginning, a middle, and an end. That's it! That's the Super3.

BEGINNING-MIDDLE-END

This seems very simple, and on the broad level it is. That's what appeals to young children. But at the same time, there's quite a bit to each part of the Super3. There are processes within processes: skills, understandings, and approaches within each part. Over time, children will learn these, moving from familiarity to mastery. For now, let's start simple in the way we introduce the Super3 to young students.

We often start by asking students to think about stories and to "imagine that you are the main character in a story." A story has 3 parts: a beginning, a middle, and an end.

① BEGINNING: Plan

What usually happens at the beginning of a story? Well, if you are the main character, you are probably going to try to figure out what you are supposed to do. What is your task or problem or quest?

Also, what will it take to complete that task? What might you have to do, what information might you need, and how will you know when you are done? These are the kinds of things that we would like children to think about and be able to do when they start a new task or assignment. In a word, in the BEGINNING, we "plan." And that's what we want children to learn to do: to Plan.

Of course, we do not expect them to be good at planning right away. That's because, as noted previously, there really is a great deal of depth to each part of the Super3. Over time, children will gain experience and abilities in each part of the Super3 process. But, the Super3 itself provides an easy and familiar pattern to remember, a guide to fall back on when they get stuck, and a process to link together various tools, procedures, and methods that they learn.

2 MIDDLE: Do

Back to our story. So now, as the main character, you have your plan. You know what you are supposed to do, the information you need, and how to proceed. Now is when you "do it." You carry out the various tasks including locate and use the information. This is the action!

The time to complete Part 2 of the Super3 can vary greatly—from a 20 minute class session to multiple days or weeks. Also, sometimes children get confused during the middle—they forget what they were supposed to do. But, with the Super3 they don't panic! They know to go back to Part 1 to remember their plan and reflect on what they were supposed to do.

1 END: Review

Now you are almost done—but not quite. Good problem-solvers know that before a task is completed, they should look back to see if they did everything that they were supposed to do. Did you complete all parts of the task? Is everything as "good" as it ought to be? Should you go back and finish something? Just as older students and adults continuously review, edit, and change their work, young children should and can do this also.

In Part 3, children learn that it is okay to review and revise; it is okay to go back and finish up. So often, assessment and review of work has a negative tone but we want children to learn that it's a good thing to review their work, to make changes, and to think about the steps they engaged in as they complete the task. We also want children to consider what they would do differently next time, so that they learn and improve.

That's it! That's the Super3.
BEGINNING: Plan
MIDDLE: Do
END: Review

Again, the Super3 is simple—it's a familiar pattern, easy for children to remember. But, "under the hood," the Super3 is complex as each part can be further broken down into a set of actions or activities. In this way, the Super3 is a valuable framework for putting various tools, procedures, and methods in a process context. Further, students do not really need to be "taught" anything new with the Super3, it is designed to be used with the current curriculum, for all subject areas, and in a variety of settings, both personal and academic.

THE SUPER3, LEARNERS, AND TEACHERS

The Super3 is designed for children in preschool through second grade. It is a spin-off from our popular and widely used Big6 approach (explained in more detail in the next chapter). While many educators and parents have successfully used the Big6 with very young children, we felt that even six stages were too many to remember. So, we developed the Super3 which links to the Big6 in the following way:

Super3	Big6
BEGINNING: Plan	Task Definition
	Information Seeking Strategies
MIDDLE: Do	Location & Access
	Use of Information
	Synthesis
END: Review	Evaluation

Figure 1.1: **Chart: Big6/Super3 Comparison**

The Super3 has been introduced by teachers and parents to children as young as the preschool age, while some continue to use the Super3 into third grade. After that, it is fairly easy to transition into the Big6 as noted above.

The Super3 helps young learners across all curriculum areas. It is widely applicable to:

- schoolwork (completing a worksheet or making a picture).
- recreation (becoming better at soccer or how to play checkers).
- decision-making in personal life (choosing a television show to watch or buying a birthday present for mom).

The magic is that children do not necessarily have to learn new content or curriculum and the Super3 can be applied to all situations. The Super3 can be and **is** fun for children to learn.

Flexibility is one of the best parts of the Super3. It is a way to talk about process, but it is flexible in area of application and also in use. As stated earlier, although the Super3 is presented in a logical order, the parts aren't necessarily linear. Children can start at any of the 3 parts (Do, Review, Plan), and most of us jump around or loop back (Plan, Do, Plan, Review, Do, Review, Do, Review). The key is to be able to successfully complete each part at some point in time.

THE SUPER3: LEARNING AND SUCCESS!

It is relatively easy to help children learn about "stuff"—about subjects, curriculum, and content such as:

- science: animals, planets and, stars.
- social studies: communities, places.
- language arts: people and their stories.
- math: addition/subtraction number families, number patterns.

We know how to teach and talk about these things. We can share facts and show pictures or videos and read from books. But, it is harder to talk about "processes"—about how to do things. At the same time, it's really important that children understand and improve their processes.

One of the most prevalent and important goals of education is for students to learn how to become better thinkers and problem-solvers. Problem solving can be defined as the thought process used to solve a problem. This often requires "critical" or "higher-level" thinking. Wikipedia.com states that "given research in cognitive psychology, educators increasingly believe that schools should focus more on teaching their students critical thinking skills than on memorizing facts by rote learning." We also see these important abilities included in reports and programs touting "21st century" or "information age" learning, for example, the Partnership for 21st Century Schools. This is an advocacy organization infusing 21st century skills into education. These skill sets include information and communication, thinking and problem solving, interpersonal and self-direction skills, global awareness, entrepreneurial skills, and civic literacy.

Learning problem-solving skills does not begin in college. Every day, even very young children tackle tasks, make decisions, and solve problems both on an academic and personal level. In the early elementary years, teachers provide opportunities for their young students to improve their thinking on a daily basis in a variety of situations. By using the Super3 and implementing the different parts into the classroom, young children are exposed to crucial problem solving skills at an early age. With practice and repetition, it is our hope that the Super3 will lay the foundation for more complex problem-solving situations.

That's what the Super3 is all about:

- Helping young students to improve their thinking and problem-solving skills.
- Helping young students to do a better job at completing tasks.
- Helping young students to recognize what they are doing.
- Helping young students to label and talk about what they are doing.

Education is about learning both content and processes. As noted above, content is fairly easy to describe, and we do so in recognizable subject areas or disciplines:

- science.
- social studies.
- language arts.
- mathematics.
- health.
- language.

There are equally familiar "topics" or "units" within these subject areas:

- animals.
- math computations.
- my community.
- planets and stars.
- states, countries, and the world we live in.

Some topics do focus on learning processes, particularly in mathematics, reading, and writing:

- addition, subtraction, multiplication, division.
- writing narrative, expository, letters, descriptive pieces.
- reading to answer specific questions.
- creating an outline.

Most teachers and parents would agree that it is easier to identify, explain, and teach content than processes. For example, we can explain or demonstrate about:

- the concepts of addition, subtraction, multiplication, and division.
- the difference between solids, liquids, and gasses.
- the five senses.
- different weather patterns.
- parts of speech including nouns, verbs, adjectives, and adverbs.
- story elements such as characters, setting, problem, and solution.

It gets more complicated when we try to help students learn to be better overall problem-solvers. Problem-solving is more than simply stringing together isolated skills. Also, different people go about problem-solving in different ways—there is not one, universal, step-by-step, prescriptive approach.

The Super3 will allow teachers to make the problem solving process:

- simple enough for kids to "get it" and remember it.
- complex enough to adequately depict the full process.
- flexible enough to allow for different approaches.
- applicable across a range of problem or task situations.

That's the Super3! And that's why it is an essential part of student learning.

BEGINNING: Plan
MIDDLE: Do
END: Review

Chapter **2**

THE SUPER3™ EXPLAINED

This chapter focuses on the nature of the Super3—the big picture as well as the details. As we have done with our explanations of the Big6, we take a top-down, broad to more specific look involving three different levels:

- The Overview Level: the Super3 as a broad process from beginning to end.
- The Super3 Parts: BEGINNING: Plan – MIDDLE: Do – END Review.
- The Details: skills, sub-skills, tools, activities, and techniques.

When we introduce the Super3 to children, we first show them the Super3 conceptually as a whole process, from beginning to end. Then, we focus on each of the 3 parts (Beginning, Middle, End) and the primary activity of each part (Plan, Do, Review). Over time, we work on skills, techniques, and tools within each part. In working with young students, we continually emphasize and reinforce this top-down context: the overall, broad Super3 process; the 3 parts; and specific skills, techniques, and tools within each part.

LEVEL 1: THE OVERVIEW LEVEL

> The Super3 is a broad process that people go through—from beginning to end—whenever they tackle an information task.

Whether we realize it or not, all of us undertake a process with every assignment or information task. Even young children go through a process—from beginning to end.

This is what we mean by the "overview" level. In this step we are just trying to get children to recognize that they go through a process when they work on tasks. As part of this, we recommend helping students to:

- Be aware that they personally go through a "beginning-middle-end" process all the time.
- Realize that it is just like being the main character in a story.
- Label that "beginning-middle-end" process the "Super3."
- Recognize that learning more about the Super3 process can help them to do a good job in completing tasks.

LEVEL 2: THE SUPER3 PARTS

The second level in the Super3 approach includes the actions of the 3 parts: Plan – Do – Review.

> 1. **BEGINNING: Plan**
> 2. **MIDDLE: Do**
> 3. **END: Review**

When students are in a situation that requires completing a task or making a decision, they go through certain actions: Plan, Do, and Review.

Plan: When students figure out what they are supposed to do and what they might need to do it, we call it Plan.

Do: When students get to work—including finding any information that they might need along the way, we refer to it as Do.

Review: When students check to see if they are done and if they did everything they were supposed to, we call it Review.

Often, young children are not even aware that they are completing these 3 parts. From experience, we find that success on a task means completing each of these parts successfully at some point in time. Sometimes children are not even aware that they are engaging in a particular part and that is fine. As students explore the Super3, they learn in time that they need to figure out what they are supposed to do, to carry out the actions necessary to complete a task, and to decide that they are, in fact, done and sometimes, to review their work.

Take a look at each of the Super3 parts in more detail.

LEVEL 3: SUPER3 DETAILS: SKILLS, SUB-SKILLS, TECHNIQUES, AND TOOLS

There are many facets in each of the Super3 parts. Again, we recommend taking a top-down approach—focusing on the details only after the students understand the broad process and can identify the 3 parts.

BEGINNING: Plan

It is obvious that when young students truly understand what they are expected to do, they have a better chance for success. Once they know where they want to go, they can figure out how they are going to get there. That is the essence of this "Beginning" stage—to figure out what children are supposed to do and to develop a plan of how to accomplish the task. This includes determining what information they need and where they are going to get that information from.

When they have a task or assignment, students need to determine what has to be done and what information will help to get the job done. We find that the number one problem students encounter is not knowing what's expected of them. There are many reasons for this including kids not paying attention, the directions are not clear, or the task is confusing. Regardless of the reason, if students do not understand what they are to do and do not understand the criteria upon which their work will be graded or assessed, they are at a tremendous disadvantage.

Through this first part of the Super3: BEGINNING: Plan, students learn to focus on the task and the information needed to complete the task.

- **Understanding the task**
- **Deciding on information needed to complete the task**

Consider the task: when students first receive an assignment or homework, they should begin to think:

- What am I supposed to do?
- What will the result look like if I do a really good job?
- How will I go about completing the job—what's my plan?

Through learning the Super3, students get better at describing or defining a task. They will be able to:

- state what is required in an assignment or task.
- select, narrow, or broaden topics.
- formulate questions based on topics and subtopics.

Once they have an idea of the assignment and what that are trying to accomplish, students can think about the information side:

- What do I need to find out about?
- How many sources will I need?
- What are some possible sources?

As they gain experience with the Super3, students will improve their skills in determining the information and sources they need. They will be able to:

- identify potential sources—books, people, computers, Internet, and Web sites.
- generate a list of potential information sources—text, human, digital—for a given assignment or task.

MIDDLE: Do

In the "Middle," students complete the various activities. This is the action and includes finding the necessary sources, reading or viewing the information in the sources, and putting it all together as a finished assignment.

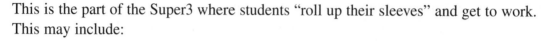

- **Locating the sources**
- **Using the information**
- **Doing the work**

This is the part of the Super3 where students "roll up their sleeves" and get to work. This may include:

- finding their information sources physically or electronically.
- finding the information in the sources.
- reading, viewing, listening.
- applying the information to the task.
- doing the actual work required.

Locating the information is easy at times but more difficult for some situations. However, it MUST be completed if your children are to succeed. Once students find the information they need, they then must be able to effectively use this information. This aspect of completing a project can frustrate students' ultimate success because they have their own set of assumptions about:

- expectations.
- usefulness of information.
- clarity of instruction.

These may get in the way of effectively using the materials they found. The Super3 tackles this aspect of student learning by focusing the learners back on the task and extracting the information that is really important to the task. This usually requires the child to: read, view, or listen; decide what is important for the particular task at hand; and finally extract the needed information. This is not always easy to do, and could certainly take a considerable amount of time.

Putting together a project or completing an assignment is a lot like baking a cake—once all the separate ingredients are identified, extraneous items put aside, and the relevant ingredients ordered and handled correctly, they need to be combined. "Do" involves organizing and presenting the information—putting it all together to finish the job. Sometimes synthesis can be as simple as recalling a specific fact, completing short answer questions, or making a decision such as deciding on a topic for a report, a product to buy, or what activity to do during free choice time. At other times, synthesis can be very complex and can involve the use of several sources, a variety of media or presentation formats, and the effective communication of abstract ideas. This is often the case with more complex activities including science projects, book reports, interviews, creating diagrams or dioramas, and writing a short story.

END: Review

Throughout the Super3 process, students are usually reflecting on where they are and how they are doing. "Review" is not meant to just be the final action that students take—a summary at the end. Evaluation is an activity that students need to get in the habit of doing all the time.

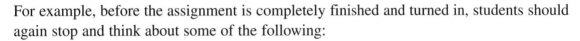

- **Checking progress**
- **Seeking help**
- **Deciding when done**
- **Reflecting on process**

For example, before the assignment is completely finished and turned in, students should again stop and think about some of the following:

- Is this done?
- Did I do what I was supposed to do?
- Do I feel OK about this?
- Should I do something else before I turn it in?
- Do I need help, and if so where can I get it?
- Was the task done or problem solved?

This is one concern in Evaluation. While working on an assignment, students can assess whether they are making progress on completing the task as defined. Sometimes they realize that they do not quite understand the task or that they need to go back and change or adjust the task. Upon completion, the students must ultimately recognize when the information problem has been solved and the quality of the result—hopefully in comparison to clearly stated criteria for judging quality. This can be done in a variety of ways including rubrics, grading checklists, self-evaluations, and peer assessment.

Lastly, we want students to reflect on personal skills and how they might do better. Students should reflect on the process and result of their work. Are they pleased with what they are doing or have competed? If they could do the project again, what might they do differently?

It is important to get students to self-assess and reflect on their performance. They need to think about their result and decide if they are pleased with it. It is not always necessary to get a top grade—sometimes okay is enough when students put forth strong efforts. At other times, they should want to strive for excellence. Young students need to understand and recognize the difference. They also need to think about the process:

- Where did they get stuck?
- Where did they waste time?

This process is helpful so that students can make the necessary changes next time. These kinds of self-reflection actions are true learning experiences. When students are self-aware, they evaluate themselves and can change their behavior for the better in the future. With teacher guidance, students may even collect and chart data on their performance in simple ways in order to improve on future assignments.

This chapter offered an extensive, top-down view of the Super3 process along with specific details about the Super3 process. The next chapter directly addresses teaching the Super3 and how to incorporate the Super3 into the classroom.

Chapter **3**

TEACHING THE SUPER3™

In the first two chapters, we emphasized that the Super3 is a 3-stage process for accomplishing tasks. We also addressed the Super3 approach—a unified, systematic approach to teaching and learning essential information and technology skills. In this chapter, we focus on methods and techniques for teaching the Super3.

INTRODUCING THE SUPER3 TO STUDENTS

When introducing the Super3 to children, we first teach them the Super3 conceptually as a broad process, from beginning to end. Next we focus on each of the 3 stages (Beginning, Middle, End) and the primary activity of each stage (Plan, Do, Review). Over time, we practice skills, techniques, and tools within each stage. In working with young students, we continually emphasize and reinforce this top-down context: the overall, broad Super3 process; the 3 stages; and specific skills, techniques, and tools within each stage.

The Super3 emphasizes the flow of the information process. Presenting the process as a story is one quick way for teachers to help students to get started or to determine where they might be having trouble. To help young learners think in terms of process, have them imagine themselves as the main character in a story about completing a specific task. Teachers may want to identify a specific character and story, such as Little Red Riding Hood for example. Now have students explain the plot line of the story and how does the character prepare to tackle the problem? After the main task is identified and described, have students consider whether the character made the best choices. Think about other ideas and options that the character may have chosen instead. These three simple steps are the Super3: Plan, Do, and Review. Once students become comfortable with identifying these elements of the Super3, make a habit of regularly asking students to identify the Super3 steps in every story read together as a class.

Young children love to be creative and are uniquely open to learning about the Super3. Of course, part of the process of learning the content and completing the task must always include an ability to evaluate. Even kindergarten students are capable of deciding how well they accomplished the task. The teacher must also be part of the evaluation process until the children are independent and effective at this skill. The teacher will want to know whether:

- the children knew how to complete the task.
- the children identified difficulties before they happened.
- the finished product met all the requirements of the task.

GENERAL GUIDELINES FOR TEACHING THE SUPER3

The Super3 can be taught in a variety of ways and situations and across all curriculum areas:

- in context with existing assignments.
- as a whole process.
- for personal things such as choosing a gift or deciding where to go on vacation.
- using the multiple intelligences.
- using props and materials with the Super3 embedded on them: posters, stickers, bookmarks, worksheets.

TROUBLESHOOTING AT EACH PART

Teachers of young children need to be prepared to trouble-shoot at each part of the Super3 process. Some of this should be done in advance by:

- arranging for appropriate materials.
- clearly stating the expectations.
- providing examples.
- planning for frequent opportunities to check for understanding and progress.

For some children, beginning a project is the hardest thing to do. They may understand what they have to do, but have no idea what the ultimate goal is or what the end result will be. These children need more than just clarifying the task. They need help with actually starting the task. Consider providing extra examples and drafts, or comparing incremental approximations with the examples.

- Can the child describe what the teacher wants?
- Can the child state why an example is poor, mediocre, or excellent?
- Can he or she identify the required elements in the examples?
- Can he or she then say what he or she intends to do to complete the task?

Some of the children will start the project with gusto, and totally lose sight of the ultimate task. They simply cannot get the job done. These students are having trouble with the middle step. To help trouble-shoot problems in the middle, teachers may want to ask their children to explain what they have done up to that point.

- Have they lost sight of their goal?
- Are they stuck in one particular place?
- What still lies ahead that needs to be completed?

Next, children need to know whether they did a high-quality job. They should not be dependent upon the teacher to know whether they were successful. Students need to be able to estimate their success before handing in the project or assignment. At the end, ask these young learners to tell how they completed the task and how well they did.

- If they were to complete this task again, what would students do differently?
- What could students have done differently that would have made it better?
- What is the best part of their finished work?
- What could they improve on for next time?

We should note that students do not always need to actually go back and do the task again. Recognizing how we would change things is sometimes enough. This is what we like to call learning.

TEACHING PART 1— BEGINNING: Plan

We must provide opportunities for students to plan to:

- learn effective and efficient ways to size up a task.
- understand what is being asked of them.
- determine the types of information they need to complete the task.
- determine appropriate sources to use.

For example, give the students the assignment and offer 2-3 samples of completed work for the assignment including one sample that is definitely poor, one that is mediocre, and one of high quality. These can be teacher-made work or examples from past students. Have the students assess the samples in terms of the assignment:

- Does it do what was required?
- Is it complete?
- How could it be improved?
- What was the best part of this assignment?

Another technique is to give less rather than more direction on assignments. Teachers often lead students through every step in an assignment—verbally or in writing. Sometimes it is necessary for teachers to be very direct and specific, but too often this is done without even thinking of the message being communicated. When teachers give a great deal of detail or step-by-step directions, they are doing most of the task definition or "planning" work. They are assuming primary responsibility for task definition and assignment planning. We want students to assume ownership and responsibility. Therefore teachers may want to gradually provide less rather than more explanation. Do not spell out much detail at all or make it a game. Just give a vague, broad description of what you want the students to do on a project, homework, or even for a test. Be willing to answer any and all questions about the assignment, but put the burden on the students to find out exactly what is expected. For example, the assignment directions might be to write a story. If this is the only directive given, students will need to ask more detailed questions about the task in order to find out more information:

- What kind of story?
- How long should the story be?
- What will the story be about?
- What materials and resources are available to use?
- When does the story need to be completed by?
- What story elements must be included in the story?

Teachers can also help by building into their classroom various brainstorming activities to identify the wide range of possible sources. For example, break the students into small groups and have each group brainstorm and narrow related to a topic, then compare results with the whole class. Or present an assignment and a list of possible sources. Then, on a card, have each student write down their source of choice and their reason for selecting that source. These then can be shared with the partners or the class. Another idea is to have a whole class brainstorming session where the class completes a concept web on the board with "possible sources" at the center of the web. Students can take turns going up to the board and writing down their different ideas.

TEACHING PART 2 — MIDDLE: Do

Teachers can help their students with "do" in lots of ways. They can help in math by teaching how to search the textbook or class notes for examples of how to solve a type of problem. They can demonstrate by example by using a back-of-the-book index while the children watch. Just recognizing text features including table of contents, glossaries, and indexes is a valuable lesson. Have students keep a log for one week of every time they used a table of contents, glossary, or index and have them record what, why, and how it was useful. Teachers can model the story writing process on the board with the whole class and can model fluent reading while reading aloud.

Many teachers already do this type of modeling, teaching, and learning with their classes. Lessons and exercises on reading, viewing, or listening for a purpose, comprehension, and note-taking all help students to develop their use of information skills. Connecting these activities to the Super3 can reinforce the role of these skills in the overall problem-solving process.

For example, consider a teacher working with students on a listening exercise and listening techniques. The students may begin to improve and grasp various listening techniques, but they really don't know when to use them or how to integrate them into their regular routine and habits. The Super3 helps by providing a familiar "process" context for the students. The teacher can explain that, "today, we are going to focus on improving our listening. We use these skills during Super3 Part 2: Do when we are listening for information." Then, whenever the students are in the "middle" or "do" part of an assignment or task that involves listening, the listening techniques can be recommended or reinforced.

Or imagine a teacher working with students on reading comprehension and key words in questions. The teacher is trying to get students to read for a purpose, to make the connection between the words in a question and the words in a passage of text. Again, the students may grasp the specific skill, but they may not know when or how to apply it. But that could change if the teacher had first made the connection to the Super3 asking, "What's the first part of the Super3? That's right—in the Beginning, we Plan." The teacher continues, "In reading for a purpose, planning means first understanding what you are looking for. One way we do that is to look for key words in our questions—before we read!"

You get the picture! The Super3 gives students a familiar context for applying their understandings, skills, and techniques within a recognizable process.

TEACHING PART 3 — END: Review

Little attention is usually paid to student self-reflection or self-assessment. Teachers are crucial to getting students involved in this review or checking part. One approach is to build in break or "time-out" reflection points during the process to check out:

- if they are clear about the assignment or task.
- how well they are doing.
- what is working and what is more difficult.

It's important for teachers to provide clear directions and criteria for assessment. This does not mean being over-detailed or elaborate. It means making sure that students understand what they are being asked to do and how they will complete the task. This can be done by having students repeat back the directions for the task verbally, write down one or two sentences about the requirements of the task, share the easiest and most difficult part of the task with their neighbor, or simply walk around while students are working and informally check in with class members.

Scoring guides or rubrics are another way to help students to assess themselves or to fully understand how they will be assessed. Ultimately, evaluation should encourage students to improve and help them to do so. These scoring guides or rubrics do not have to be complicated or elaborate. Sometimes a simple checklist works, or a questionnaire where students comment on their work. Examples of these are in the "Review" section of the next chapter.

In the Super3 approach, Review encourages students to gauge their own progress, strengths, and skills in a way that is useful to their continued learning. Evaluation is the culmination of the entire process, but it is often the part of the process that receives the least attention. Teachers should carefully consider activities and exercises to emphasize Review. These can be informal or formal, simple or more complex, and whole class, small group, or individual.

For example, teachers can do a whole class modeling activity where they take a completed assignment and use a checklist to check for things such as name and date on the paper, sentences begin with capital letter, punctuation at the end of each sentence, and the work is neat and complete. Students can then use this checklist before they turn in their work. At the end of an assignment, teachers could have students share their best part of the assignment and the hardest part of the assignment in their journals. When implementing such activities, teachers are actually helping students in every part of the Super3.

Chapter **4**

SUPER3™ WORKSHEETS

HOW TO USE THE WORKSHEETS

This chapter offers dozens of worksheets designed to help young learners become more familiar with the Super3 process. With teacher instruction, modeling, and guidance, the worksheets will help students to:

- improve their thinking and problem-solving skills.
- become more efficient and effective at completing tasks.
- recognize what they are doing and the importance of it.

As they complete the worksheets over time, students will become more and more proficient in basic problem solving skills and it will really begin to reflect in their work. Increasingly, students will be able to describe their actions in terms of the Super3 process. This is self-awareness or "meta-cognition" and it allows students to make the connection between various tools, techniques, and activities and a commonly known and used process—the Super3.

The worksheets do not have to be used sequentially or in a linear manner. In addition, not all worksheets will be applicable to all assignments or subject areas. It is expected that teachers and learners will jump around, focusing on one specific skill at a time. Each worksheet can be adapted or modified for all types of learners. For students who are just learning how to write, teachers may want to have students dictate their thoughts and ideas for some worksheets. Another option is for students to draw pictures or cut pictures out from magazines to include on the worksheets. Each worksheet can be personalized to meet your instructional needs as well as tailored to meet the needs of the different learners in you classroom.

WHEN USING A GIVEN WORKSHEET, WE RECOMMEND THE FOLLOWING PROCESS

1 Discuss the curriculum and assignment context.
- Introduce or restate the curriculum context to the students.
- Introduce or restate the specific classroom assignment on which the students are working.

2 Discuss the Super3 process.
- In terms of the assignment, where are students in the Super3 process?
- Explain what students are trying to accomplish.
- Explain the next steps for students.

3 Introduce the Super3 worksheet and make the connection to the curriculum/context.
- What Super3 stage is the focus for this task and worksheet?
- Why is it the focus?
- What are the standards and objectives?
- What do the students have to do?
- Why are students doing this? How will it benefit them?
- Discuss the expected outcome or give an example of what the result should look like.

4 Evaluate and debrief on the worksheet and process.
- What did students learn?
- How difficult was it to complete the worksheet?
- Do students need more instruction or follow-up?

GUIDE TO INDIVIDUAL WORKSHEETS

While many uses of the worksheets are readily apparent, we offer additional information related to intent, use, evaluation, and special tips. In the introduction to each worksheet chapter, we offer explanations for each worksheet in terms of:

- Objective/Purpose.
- Context for Use.
- Outcome.
- Tips.

We also provide a short narrative section of ideas for teaching and learning based on our experiences with young children, the Super3, and the worksheets. "Ideas for Teaching and Learning" is intended to help teachers get started right away but also to offer suggestions for multiple or alternative uses.

Worksheets for

Super3 Process

Worksheet

The Super3: Process 1

- **Objective/Purpose:** Students will identify the overall Super3 process: beginning, middle, and end; plan, do, review.
- **Context for Use:** For use when students are beginning a new project, task, or assignment.
- **Outcome:** Student responses will include specific details from the BEGINNING: Plan, MIDDLE: Do, END: Review.
- **Tips:** Let children draw pictures for this worksheet and then dictate their ideas to you.

IDEAS FOR TEACHING AND LEARNING

This worksheet can be used as a planning sheet for students to complete before they do the required task or project. It may be helpful to guide students with the following questions.

BEGINNING: Plan

- What is my job or task?
- What will I do to complete the assignment?
- What do I need in order to complete the assignment?

MIDDLE: Do

- How will I "do" my work?
- How will I show what I have learned?
- How will I present my work?

END: Review

- How will I review or check my work before I turn it in?
- How will I know if I completed the assignment?

Super3
• Plan
• Do
• Review

Name:______________________________

Process 1

PROCESS CHART

BEGINNING: Plan

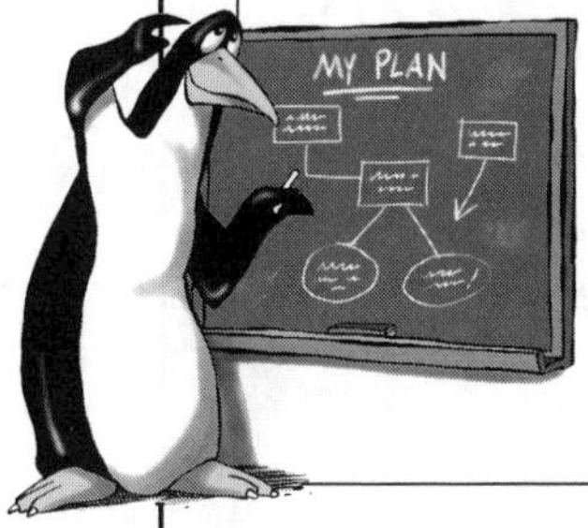

MIDDLE: Do

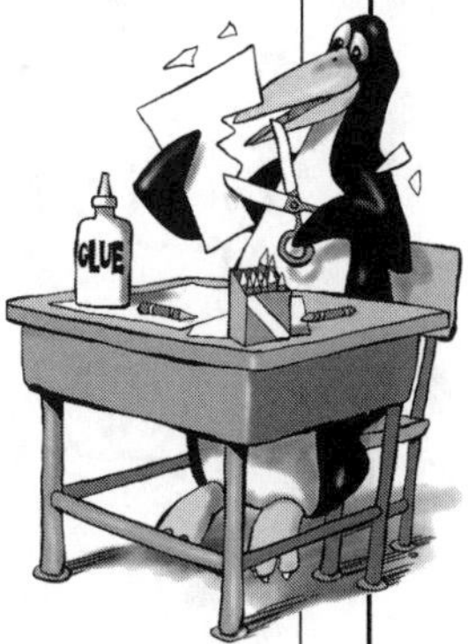

END: Review

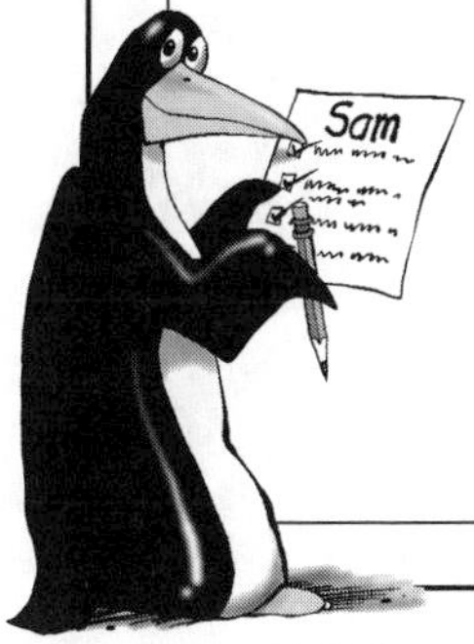

Figure 4.1 **Process 1**

Process 1

PROCESS CHART

BEGINNING: Plan

I need to make a map of my neighborhod.

MIDDLE: Do

Draw my neighborhod on poster board

Label streets and buildings

END: Review

Check my work
Did I do everything
I needed to?

Figure 4.2 **Process 1 example**

Worksheet
The Super3: Process 2

- **Objective/Purpose:** Students will outline and plan their assignment before beginning the actual task.
- **Context for Use:** For use when a new task or assignment is given.
- **Outcome:** Student responses will show that they know what they need to do in order to complete the assignment and how they will go about doing it.
- **Tips:** By doing this exercise repeatedly, students will improve in their understanding of the Super3 process, teachers' directions, and their ability to identify the task at hand. It allows learners to make a plan before they start their work.

IDEAS FOR TEACHING AND LEARNING

This is a simple worksheet that focuses on the process of completing a task or assignment. It allows students to think deeper about their assignment and how they will complete it.

Process 2

Before I start I will_____

_____

_____

_____.

In order to complete this assignment I will_____

_____

_____

_____.

I will know my job is complete when_____

_____

_____

_____.

Figure 4.3 **Process 2**

Process 2

Before I start I will _think about the numbers I want to use and decide on + or − for my story problems._

In order to complete this assignment I will _write 4 story problems. 2 will be +, 2 will be −. And solve them and draw a picture._

1. $25 + 25 = 50$ 3. $62 - 10 = 52$

2. $42 + 24 = 66$ 4. $99 - 11 = 88$

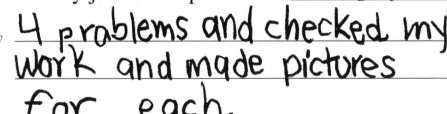

I will know my job is complete when _I did my 4 problems and checked my work and made pictures for each._

Figure 4.4 **Process 2 example**

Worksheets for

BEGINNING:
Plan

Worksheet
The Super3: Plan 1

- **Objective/Purpose:** Students will identify their task and what they need to do.
- **Context for Use:** For use when any task or assignment is given.
- **Outcome:** Student responses will show that they completely understand their job.
- **Tips:** By doing this exercise repeatedly, students will improve in their understanding of teachers' directions and ability to identify the task at hand.

IDEAS FOR TEACHING AND LEARNING

This is a simple worksheet that focuses on the "job at hand." One way to introduce the worksheet is to talk about jobs and workers and how people get things done. Then, it's helpful to make the connection between "jobs" and "tasks:" in order to complete a job, you may have lots of tasks. You can give examples of this:

Building a house means:

- clearing and digging for the foundation.
- pouring cement.
- building the frame.
- putting on the roof and the siding.
- putting in the plumbing and the electricity.
- finishing the inside walls and floors.

A doctor's job is to:

- give check-ups to healthy kids.
- diagnose illnesses.
- helps sick kids feel better.

We are trying to get students to realize that they too have jobs and tasks. To do a good job, it really helps to think about ahead of time about the job and the tasks. Figuring out what you have to do to complete the task is an important step.

This worksheet is an easy, first effort to focus attention on tasks.

Super3
- Plan
- Do
- Review

Name:____________________________________

Plan 1

What is my job and what do I need to do?

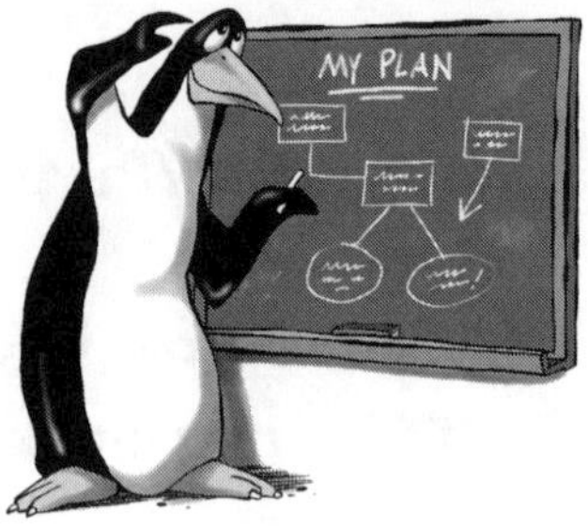

Figure 4.6 **Plan 1**

Name:_____

Plan 1

What is my job and what do I need to do?

cat

I need to pick a
animal and reserch it.
I have to draw a
picture and write 3 facts.

Figure 4.6 **Plan 1 example**

Worksheet

The Super3: Plan 2

- **Objective/Purpose:** Students will set goals for themselves in each academic area.
- **Context for Use:** For use in the beginning of the year and periodically throughout the year.
- **Outcome:** Students will outline specific learning goals that they would like to accomplish.
- **Tips:** This worksheet can be completed individually or with the teacher. Teacher and student should review and update this periodically throughout the year. Teacher should help students to keep goals realistic and attainable. This is a great worksheet to share with families and use during parent-teacher conferences.

IDEAS FOR TEACHING AND LEARNING

This worksheet is a more detailed approach to looking at the "job" of being a student. Here, students are asked to begin to think broadly about their tasks in the different areas:

- reading.
- writing.
- science.
- math.

In this education world where differentiation is essential in the classroom setting, creating personal goals allows teachers and students to individualize instruction appropriate for them. Students will be able to reflect on their learning and set learning targets for themselves. By doing this, students have specific goals to work towards and are more motivated to learn. Students are taking responsibility of their learning and are able to learn at their pace.

Name:_____________________________

Super3
- **Plan**
- **Do**
- **Review**

Plan 2

My goals for reading are____________________________

____

____

____.

My goals for writing are____________________________

____

____

____.

My goals for math are______________________________

____

____

____.

My goals for science are________________________

____

____

____.

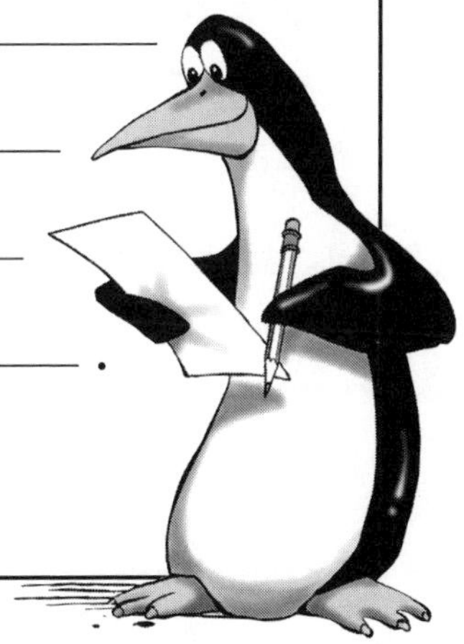

Figure 4.7 **Plan 2**

Name:_____

Plan 2

My goals for reading are to memorize the sight words.

My goals for writing are write a story about a magic kingdom.

My goals for math are do multiplication.

My goals for science are explore rocks and study volcanos.

Figure 4.8 **Plan 2 example**

From The Super3™: Information Skills for Younger Learners by Laura Eisenberg Robinson and Michael B. Eisenberg. Columbus, OH: Linworth Publishing, Inc. Further reproduction prohibited. Copyright © 2007.

Worksheet
The Super3: Plan 3

- **Objective/Purpose:** Students will identify exactly what they need in order to complete the task.
- **Context for Use:** For use when students are deciding what they need in order to get the task done.
- **Outcome:** Students will know what resources they need to complete the task.
- **Tips:** Teacher may want to briefly discuss each option beforehand and provide examples of what "other" sources may be needed (magazines, music, newspaper).

IDEAS FOR TEACHING AND LEARNING

While the previous 2 worksheets focus on the task, this one focuses on "resources." There are 4 basic types of resources that students will use for most tasks:

- people.
- books.
- computer resources.
- self.

Name:_____

Plan 3

What will I need to complete my task?

Computer 	Art Supplies 	Books 

Teacher 	Family/Friends 	Paper/Pencil 

Other:	Other:	Other:

Figure 4.9 **Plan 3**

From The Super3™: Information Skills for Younger Learners by Laura Eisenberg Robinson and Michael B. Eisenberg. Columbus, OH: Linworth Publishing, Inc. Further reproduction prohibited. Copyright © 2007.

Name:_____

Plan 3

What will I need to complete my task?

Computer   Art Supplies    Books

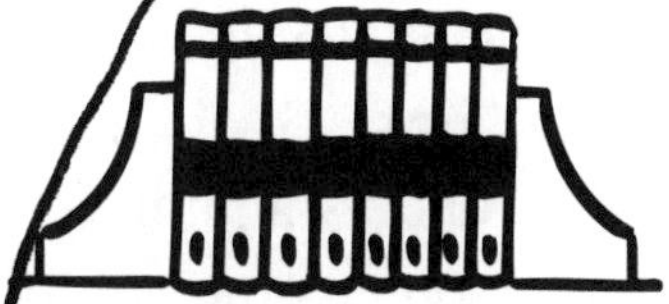

Teacher    Family/Friends    Paper/Pencil

Other: Other: Other:

magazines

Figure 4.10 **Plan 3 example**

From The Super3™: Information Skills for Younger Learners by Laura Eisenberg Robinson and Michael B. Eisenberg. Columbus, OH: Linworth Publishing, Inc. Further reproduction prohibited. Copyright © 2007.

Worksheet

The Super3: Plan 4

- **Objective/Purpose:** Students will identify their task for the project and the sources they might use.
- **Context for Use:** For use when any task or assignment is given.
- **Outcome:** Student responses will show that they know what to do and the sources they might use.
- **Tips:** By doing this exercise repeatedly, students will improve in their understanding of teachers' directions and ability to independently select sources they might need in order to complete the task.

This worksheet is helpful when getting students to look at their project as a whole. It allows children to see the big picture and to plan before diving into their task. By doing this pre-planning, we hope that students will critically think about what they need to do and what sources they need in order to complete the project.

This worksheet is helpful when students have to do a "mini-research project" or find information on a specific topic.

Examples may include:

- What is your favorite animal? Write or Draw three facts about this animal.

- Create a new book cover for a book you have recently read. Include pictures of at least 1 character and the setting of the story.

- Pick a state in the United States and create a travel brochure about this state. Include a map of the state, the climate of the state, and at least 3 things you might do while visiting this state.

- Create a map and set of directions going from the school to your house.

Name:____________________________________

Super3
- **Plan**
- **Do**
- **Review**

Plan 4

For this project I need to______________________________

____

____

____

____.

• • • •

The sources I might use are____________________________

____

____

____

____.

• • • •

The supplies I need are_______________________________

____

____

____

____

____

____.

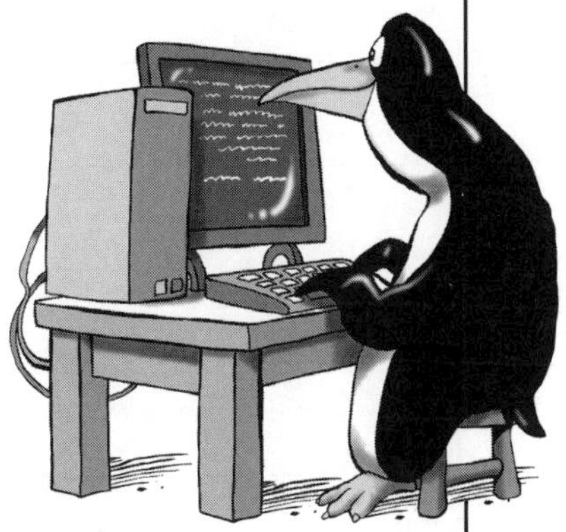

Figure 4.11 **Plan 4 example**

Super3
- Plan
- Do
- Review

Name: ____________________

Plan 4

For this project I need to ____________________
make a book about
me and my life
.

• • • •

The sources I might use are me, my mom
and dad and brother
baby book
photo album
.

• • • •

The supplies I need are paper books
pencil pictures
ME!
.

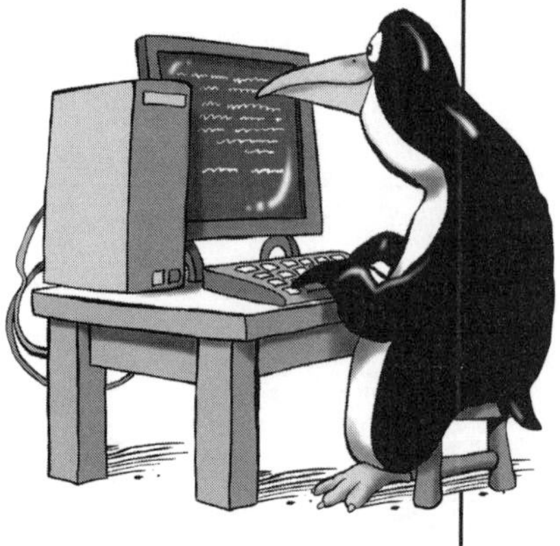

Figure 4.12 **Plan 4**

Worksheet
The Super3: Plan 5

- **Objective/Purpose:** Students will brainstorm and identify all possible sources where they might get the information needed.
- **Context for Use:** For use when students are deciding what sources they can use to get the information they need.
- **Outcome:** Students will select all possible sources where they can find the information.
- **Tips:** This worksheet encourages students to work outside their comfort zone and learn to make use of a variety of different sources. Before you get started, it will be helpful to talk about each source and the context for using it.

IDEAS FOR TEACHING AND LEARNING

This worksheet is an efficient tool to use when students have to actually gather or find information for a specific assignment. It will help students think about the sources that are available to them and help them to determine the best source to use to find the information they need.

Ideas for topics might include:

- Where would you find information about the state you live in?

- Where is the United States located on Earth?

- What is a doctor's job?

- What does the word "excitement" mean?

- How many planets are in the solar system?

- Current Events: What is something you could do this weekend? Or, What is something that happened in our world today?

Name:_____

Plan 5

For this assignment, I might get my information from:

Dictionary

Computer

Storybook

Pictures

Family

Magazines

Friends

Encyclopedia

Newspaper

Non-Fiction Books

Teacher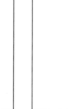

Map or Globe

Other:

Other:

Other:

Figure 4.13 **Plan 5**

Plan 5

For this assignment, I might get my information from:

Dictionary

Computer

Storybook

Pictures

Family

Magazines

Friends

Encyclopedia

Newspaper

Non-Fiction Books

Teacher

Map or Globe

Other:

Other:

Other:

Figure 4.14 **Plan 5 example**

Worksheet

The Super3: Plan 6

- **Objective/Purpose:** Students will identify 3 goals they have for the school.
- **Context for Use:** For use in the beginning of the school year when students are asked to reflect on the current school year.
- **Outcome:** Students will think about their school year and identify 3 goals they want to accomplish.
- **Tips:** Try to encourage students to think BIG, and not just about the academic areas. What about being a good friend (and encourage students to think even deeper by asking guiding questions such as: What does a good friend do? How does a good friend act?) or learning a new sport or hobby? It is valuable (and fun) to review goals with students and families at both the beginning and end of the school year to discuss progress.

Have students write, draw pictures, or cut out images from magazines that depict their goals.

IDEAS FOR TEACHING AND LEARNING

This open-ended goal setting page can be used by students to create goals 3 goals for the school year. These goals do not necessarily need to be focused on academics.

Possible goals include:

- Social goals:
    - make 5 new friends.
    - ask a peer to join in a game.
- Communication goals:
    - use kind words to kids and adults.
    - use please and thank-you.
    - raise hand before speaking.
    - no interruptions.
- Citizenship goals:
    - Clean up trash and litter.
    - Be in charge of recycling.
- Learn to:
    - tie a shoe.
    - zip coat.
    - play soccer.
    - play the piano.
    - move up to the next belt in karate.
    - tap dance.

Super3
- Plan
- Do
- Review

Name:________________________________

Plan 6

My goals for the school year are:

1

2

3

Figure 4.15 **Plan 6**

Name:_____

Plan 6

My goals for the school year are:

1 Read more books.

2 add +   subtract

$$\begin{array}{r} 5 \\ +\ 5 \\ \hline 10 \end{array}$$ $8 - 4 = 4$

3 make 2 new friends.

Figure 4.16 **Plan 6 example**

Worksheets for
MIDDLE: Do

Worksheet

The Super3: Do 1

Super3
- Plan
- Do
- Review

- **Objective/Purpose:** Students will identify who, what, why, when, and where something happened.
- **Context for Use:** For use when students are trying to explain or tell when a specific event happened or when asked to provide a summary of a story.
- **Outcome:** Student responses will include specific details from the event and show that they understand what happened.
- **Tips:** This is an excellent activity to use when reading narrative stories. This also can be used in the classroom when conflicts arise between students. This can be used as a whole class activity, in pairs or small groups, or individually.

IDEAS FOR TEACHING AND LEARNING

When students are working on a specific task or assignment, such as retelling the events of a story or writing a personal story, it is helpful to have them think about the five W's:

1. who.
2. what.
3. where.
4. why.
5. when.
6. plus how.

By completing this worksheet, students will be able to plan and organize their thoughts and ideas in a coherent and organized manner.

For example:

Goldilocks and the Three Bears

What: Three bears went for a walk and a little girl came into their house.
Who: Goldilocks, Mama Bear, Papa Bear, Baby Bear.
Why: Goldilocks wanted to see the bears' house and to try out their possessions.
When: Morning.
Where: In the woods, the Three Bear's house.

A conflict between students:

What: Sara took the ball I was using away from me.
Who: Sara, Clare.
Why: Sara wanted a ball and there weren't any more so she took mine.
When: This morning during recess.
Where: We were playing on the playground by the basketball hoops.

Super3
- **Plan**
- **Do**
- **Review**

Name:__________________________________

Do 1

What happened?

Why did it happen?

When did it happen?

Who was there?

Where did it happen?

Figure 4.17 **Do 1**

Name:_____

Do 1

What happened?

Alex took my ball.

Why did it happen?

Alex wanted a ball and he stole mine.

When did it happen?

At morning recess on Monday 5\1\07

Who was there?

Mr. Baeder
Josie, Jack Joe

Where did it happen?

playground by the  hoop

---

Figure 4.18 **Do 1 example**

Worksheet

The Super3: Do 2

- **Objective/Purpose:** Students will use the 5 senses to describe something specific.
- **Context for Use:** For use when students are trying use their senses to describe something in detail.
- **Outcome:** Student responses will include specific observations based on the 5 senses.
- **Tips:** This can be used as an outline for a descriptive writing piece or during a science experiment. It is interesting to see how different students perceive the same thing.

IDEAS FOR TEACHING AND LEARNING

Students enjoy completing this sensory activity and using senses to explore objects, people, and their surroundings. This can also be used numerous times to compare different items: apples, oranges, and bananas; or water in the form of a solid, liquid, and gas.

This worksheet can easily be tied into learning standards in all content areas. Contexts for Use:

- Nature Walk.
- Classroom.
- Cafeteria.
- Playground.
- Describe a classmate.
- Describe an animal the class is studying.

After students complete the chart, have them use their notes to form a descriptive or expository writing piece. Half the work is already done as their main information is right there in front of them.

Super3
- **Plan**
- **Do**
- **Review**

Do 2

Touch (feeling)

Smell (smelling)

Sound (hearing)

Sight (seeing)

Taste (tasting)

Figure 4.19 **Do 2**

From The Super3™: Information Skills for Younger Learners by Laura Eisenberg Robinson and Michael B. Eisenberg. Columbus, OH: Linworth Publishing, Inc. Further reproduction prohibited. Copyright © 2007.

Name:______________________________

Super3
- Plan
- Do
- Review

Do 2

APPLE

Touch (feeling)

smooth
hard

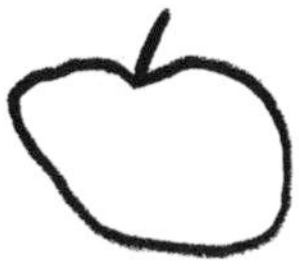

Smell (smelling)

fruity fresh

Sound (hearing)

crunchy when I bite it

Sight (seeing)

deep red
shiny brown little stem

Taste (tasting)

sweet
sour

crisp and fresh

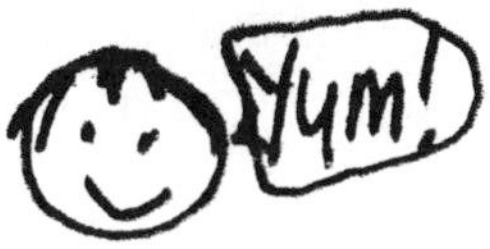

Figure 4.20 **Do 2 example**

Worksheet

The Super3: Do 3

- **Objective/Purpose:** Students will complete the thinking web with the main idea/concept in the middle and 4 details in the outlined areas.
- **Context for Use:** For use when students are explaining details about a specific concept.
- **Outcome:** Students will complete the thinking web with accurate information around a central idea/theme.
- **Tips:** This is a great worksheet to use as a pre-writing activity or when discussing main ideas versus details.

IDEAS FOR TEACHING AND LEARNING

The ideas for thinking webs are endless! Here are a few to get you started.

- Whole class activity when introducing a new topic. Teacher presents the concept to students and students share their prior knowledge about the topic. This allows the teacher to identify what the students already know about a specific concept.

- As a pre-writing activity, learners can write the main idea in the center and add their story details in the surrounding bubbles.

- This can be used when planning a class party or a field trip. Event is listed in the center with details of the event surrounding it.

- A specific character's name is in the center and students write different character traits in the outlying areas.

- A math or science term is written in the center and students define the term in the adjoining spaces. This can informally assess students' understanding of a specific term or concept.

Name:_____

Do 3

Thinking Web

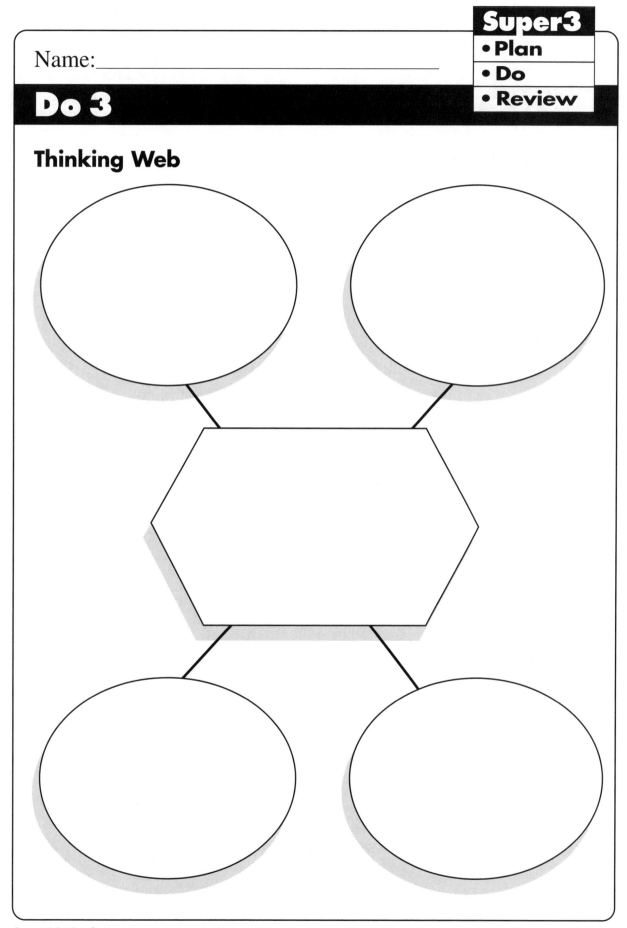

Figure 4.21 **Do 3**

Do 3

Thinking Web

has 1. 1 sister
1 dog
2 birds
Friend Niel

2. likes soccer and Karate

Jack in The big race

3. 8 year old 2 grade

4. lives in town by pool and school

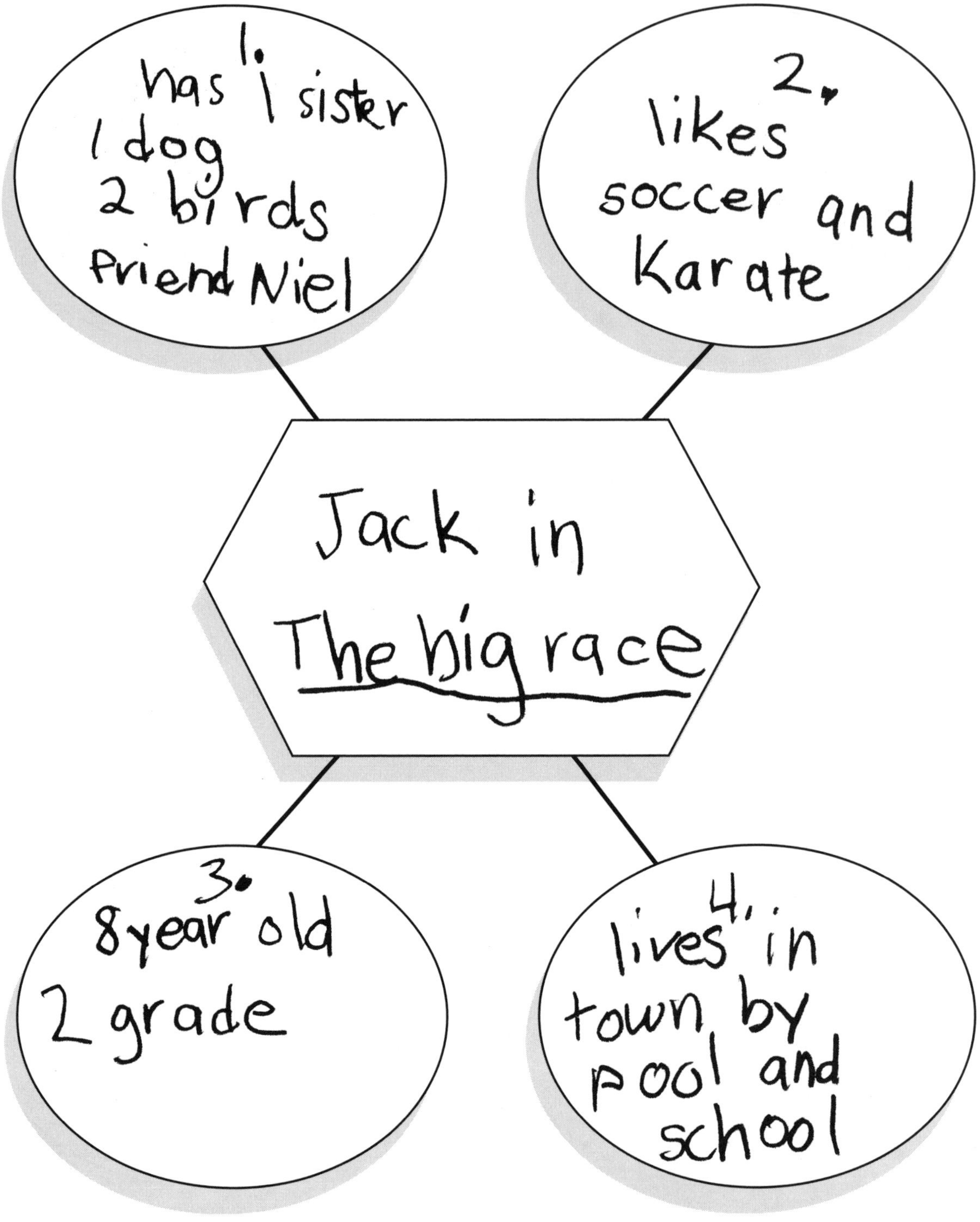

Figure 4.22 **Do 3 example**

From The Super3™: Information Skills for Younger Learners by Laura Eisenberg Robinson and Michael B. Eisenberg. Columbus, OH: Linworth Publishing, Inc. Further reproduction prohibited. Copyright © 2007.

Worksheet

The Super3: Do 4

- **Objective/Purpose:** Students will write an addition and subtraction math equation and will draw a picture depicting the equation.
- **Context for Use:** For use when students are learning math facts and when they are asked to explain their mathematical thinking.
- **Outcome:** Students will correctly write 2 math equations and will show their thinking in pictures, words, or numbers.
- **Tips:** For this activity, students should be encouraged to show their mathematical thinking using words, numbers, or pictures. This can be used in a variety of ways: teacher gives students the sum/difference and students create the equation or teacher gives students the numbers and they have to determine the sum/difference.

IDEAS FOR TEACHING AND LEARNING

So many of today's state assessments want students to explain their thinking using words, numbers, and pictures. This open-ended math worksheet allows students to write a math equation and draw a picture to demonstrate their understanding.

This can be used in a variety of ways:

- Teacher dictates the math equation to students.
- Teacher can give students the answer and students need to determine the problem.
- Students create their own equations.
- Students can show the relationship between number families (e.g. $5+2 = 7$, $7-2 = 5$).

Super3
- **Plan**
- **Do**
- **Review**

Name:__________________________________

Do 4

Math Problems

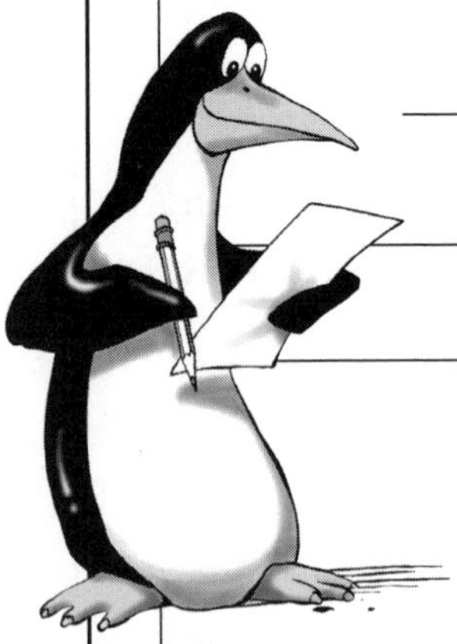

__________ + __________ = __________

__________ + __________ = __________

Figure 4.23 **Do 4**

Do 4

Math Problems

Double

$$6 + 6 = 12$$

Double + 1

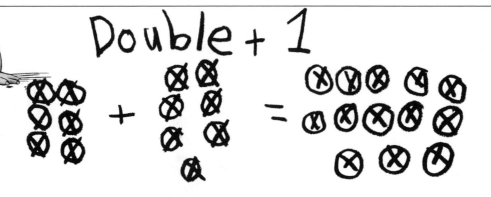

$$6 + 7 = 13$$

Figure 4.24 **Do 4 example**

Worksheet
The Super3: Do 5

- **Objective/Purpose:** Students will identify the beginning, middle, and end of a story.
- **Context for Use:** For use when students are trying to retell or summarize a story. This is a good tool to use to determine if students comprehend what they are reading.
- **Outcome:** Student responses will include specific details from the beginning, middle, and end of a story.
- **Tips:** Let children draw pictures for this worksheet and then dictate their ideas to you. This can be done with the teacher reading aloud or when students are reading independently.

IDEAS FOR TEACHING AND LEARNING

We often require students to do book reports on stories they have read. The following five worksheets provide different formats, approaches, and content for book reports. Teachers can first model and guide through completing each worksheet. Later, students can choose which book report framework they prefer.

This specific worksheet can be used as an informal assessment to determine if students understand the events of a story. It ties into national standards and helps with summarizing, sequence of events, main ideas versus details, and progression of story structure.

Name:______________________________

Super3
- **Plan**
- **Do**
- **Review**

Do 5

Story Chart

BEGINNING

MIDDLE

END

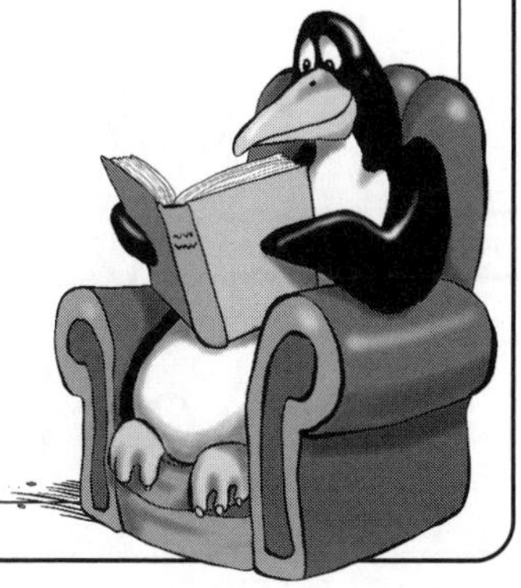

Figure 4.25 **Do 5**

Super3
- **Plan**
- **Do**
- **Review**

Do 5

Story Chart

BEGINNING

Jack had a soccer game. He wanted to win.

#1

MIDDLE

He practiced with his team and his brother. He got rest.

END

Jack tried his best. His team won because Jack scored the last goal.

Figure 4.26 **Do 5 example**

Worksheet
The Super3: Do 6

- **Objective/Purpose:** Students will identify basic story elements of a story: characters, setting, story structure: beginning, middle, end.
- **Context for Use:** For use when students are trying to learn basic story elements and demonstrate story comprehension.
- **Outcome:** Students will identify characters and setting of the story and retell the story with a beginning, middle, and end.
- **Tips:** This can be used as an informal assessment to determine if students comprehend what they read. This also can be used as a book report form.

IDEAS FOR TEACHING AND LEARNING

The worksheet is a more detailed story map that can be used for fiction stories. It breaks down the story elements and allows students to gain an understanding of the whole story while targeting the story elements.

Name:______________________________

Super3

- **Plan**
- **Do**
- **Review**

Do 6

Story Map

Title: ______________________________

Author: ______________________________

SETTING

CHARACTER

BEGINNING

MIDDLE

END

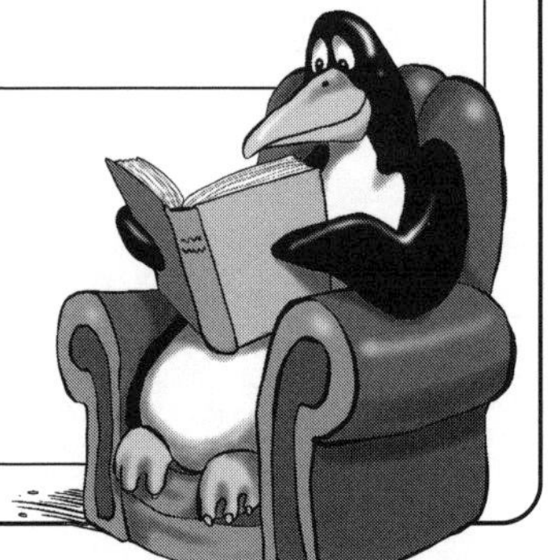

Figure 4.27 **Do 6**

Name:_____

Do 6

Story Map

Title: <u>In the Deep Woods</u>

Author: <u>John Nolan</u>

SETTING Vermont mountains in summer, forest campsite   Lake Long

CHARACTER
Lee - 9 years old   Manager - Doug
Mom, Dad   cousins - Jordan - 10
brother - Ty - 2   sister - Misa - 6

BEGINNING   Lee went to camp with family.

MIDDLE   They hiked, played ball, saw a bear, swam.

END   They all slept on the way home.

Figure 4.28 **Do 6 example**

Worksheet

The Super3: Do 7

- **Objective/Purpose:** Students will identify the basic elements of a story.
- **Context for Use:** For use when students have to identify the specific elements of a story.
- **Outcome:** Students will demonstrate comprehension of the story by recording the different story elements.
- **Tips:** Students can either draw pictures, write, or do a combination of both for their responses.

IDEAS FOR TEACHING AND LEARNING

This worksheet ties into national learning standards for reading and will help students to distinguish between the different story elements. This worksheet can be used as an informal assessment to determine student understanding of story elements.

Super3
- **Plan**
- **Do**
- **Review**

Name: ______________________________

Do 7

Story Elements

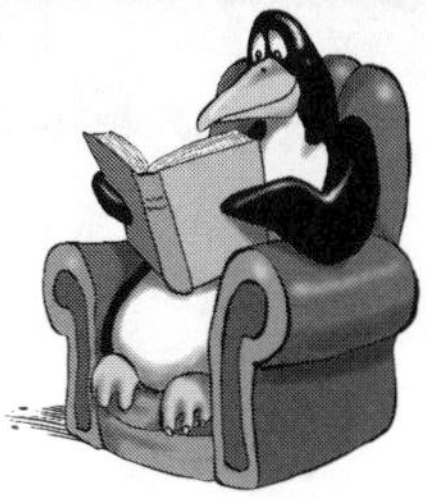

Title: ______________________________

CHARACTERS	SETTING

PROBLEM	SOLUTION

Figure 4.29 **Do 7**

Do 7

Story Elements

Title: Where did the magic go?

CHARACTERS	SETTING
Harry Julia cat Cleo pesky baby Juan	backyard of Harrys house Summer Day

PROBLEM	SOLUTION
Harry can't do his magic tricks or find his magic book	He has to look all over, go to the library, and then he finds his book and can do tricks.

Figure 4.30 **Do 7 example**

Worksheet
The Super3: Do 8

- **Objective/Purpose:** Students will identify the main idea and details for a given topic.
- **Context for Use:** For use with fiction or non-fiction text when trying to distinguish between main ideas and details. This can be used as an outline for writing a summary.
- **Outcome:** Student responses will include the main idea with supporting details.
- **Tips:** This is a great activity to use with non-fiction text. It can be used as a note-taking worksheet when students are reading or as an assessment for after students have completed the reading.

IDEAS FOR TEACHING AND LEARNING

This worksheet is an effective learning tool to use when teaching students the difference between the main idea and details. Further, it can be copied and used numerous times throughout a story. It works with both fiction and non-fiction texts.

Super3
- **Plan**
- **Do**
- **Review**

Name:______________________________

Do 8

MAIN IDEA

DETAILS	DETAILS	DETAILS

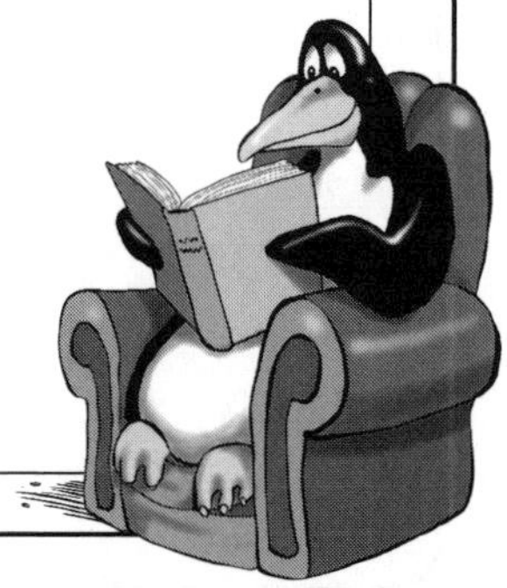

Figure 4.31 **Do 8**

Super3
- **Plan**
- **Do**
- **Review**

Do 8

MAIN IDEA

stars are balls of burning gas.

DETAILS

hot fire

DETAILS

millons of miles away

DETAILS

colors red yellow orange

Figure 4.32 **Do 8 example**

Worksheet
The Super3: Do 9

- **Objective/Purpose:** Students will select a character and describe specific characteristics about him/her.
- **Context for Use:** For use when completing a character study about a specific story character.
- **Outcome:** Student responses will include specific details about the character.
- **Tips:** It's fun to model this activity using class members, school staff, or the principal.

IDEAS FOR TEACHING AND LEARNING

An extension activity is to have "character day" where students dress up as their character and give a mini-presentation as their character. If the whole class has read the story, another idea is for students to share their completed worksheet with the class and have class members guess who their character is.

Name:_____

Do 9

Character: _____

What does the character say?	What do others say about the character?

What does the character look like?	How do I feel about the character?

Figure 4.33 **Do 9**

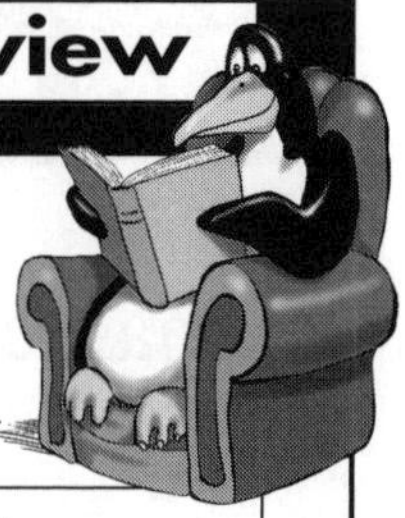

Name:_____

Do 9

Character: Juan - brother 2

What does the character say?

play with me,
I wanna help,
Do more again,
NO! NO!

What do others say about the character?

Older kids say he is a pest,
Mom says he just wants to be like the kids,

What does the character look like?

Face is always dirty,
Dark hair, big brown eyes

How do I feel about the character?

He is cute,
He is annoying,
He's only 2 so he can't help it,

Figure 4.34 **Do 9 example**

Worksheets for
END:
Review

The Super3: Review 1

- **Objective/Purpose:** Students will reflect on their work and identify their favorite part and the hardest part of the assignment.
- **Context for Use:** For use when students have completed a task or assignment as a self-assessment exercise.
- **Outcome:** Students will evaluate their own work.
- **Tips:** Have children draw pictures to go along with their responses.

IDEAS FOR TEACHING AND LEARNING

This reflection worksheet is useful after students turn in an assignment to reflect on the overall assignment. It works well to complete this individually, in pairs, or small groups.

Name:____________________________________

Super3
- **Plan**
- **Do**
- **Review**

Review 1

My favorite part of this assignment was ______________

____

____.

The hardest part of this assignment was ______________

____

____.

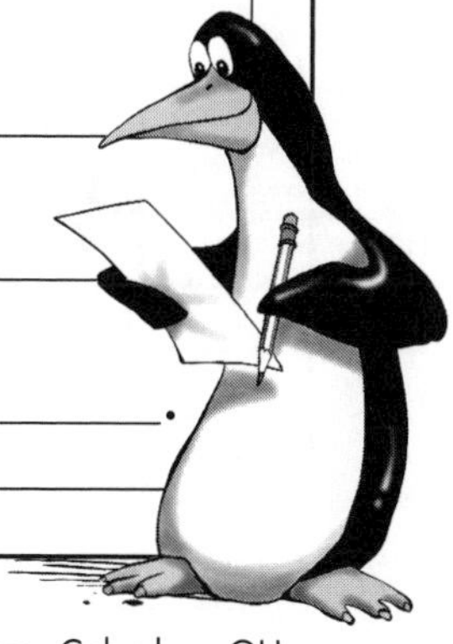

Figure 4.35 **Review 1**

Name:_____

Review 1

My favorite part of this assignment was using the computer to get details.

The hardest part of this assignment was deciding the animal to reserch.

Figure 4.36 **Review 1 example**

Worksheet

The Super3: Review 2

- **Objective/Purpose:** Students will complete a simple rating once their assignment is complete.
- **Context for Use:** For use when students have completed a task or assignment as a self-assessment exercise.
- **Outcome:** Students will evaluate their own work and how they completed the task.
- **Tips:** It is helpful complete a few examples as a whole class first to outline teacher expectations.

IDEAS FOR TEACHING AND LEARNING

Set up a policy in your classroom where students have to complete this quick and easy checklist at least 2 times a week before turning in an assignment.

Name:_____

Review 2

I followed all directions.

I found all the information I needed.

I answered all questions.

I did my best work.

I checked my work for mistakes.

Figure 4.37 **Review 2**

Name:_____

Review 2

I followed all directions.

I found all the information I needed.

I answered all questions.

I did my best work.

I checked my work for mistakes.

Figure 4.38 **Review 2 example**

Worksheet

The Super3: Review 3

- **Objective/Purpose:** Students will complete this checklist after a writing assignment before they hand in their work.
- **Context for Use:** For use before students turn in a completed writing task.
- **Outcome:** Students will reread and check their work, making any necessary changes.
- **Tips:** This is a helpful checklist for students who do not generally proofread their work and for those who rush to get their work done. Try having students work in pairs with this checklist to edit each other's work.

IDEAS FOR TEACHING AND LEARNING

This editing checklist should be used before students turn in *any* major writing assignment. Teachers may want to have this readily available in the classroom available for student use.

Name:______________________________

Super3
- **Plan**
- **Do**
- **Review**

Review 3

- [ ] I read my piece to myself.
- [ ] My writing makes sense.
- [ ] My name and the date are on my writing.
- [ ] I have a title for my writing.
- [ ] I used periods, question marks, and exclamation marks.
- [ ] I used capital letters.
- [ ] My final work is neat.
- [ ] This is my best work.

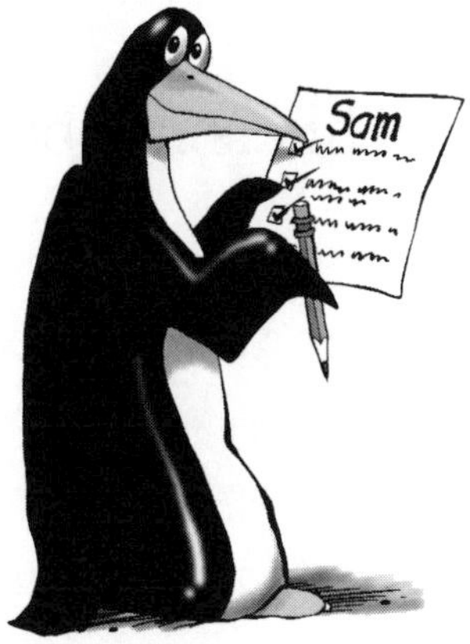

Figure 4.39 **Review 3**

Super3
- **Plan**
- **Do**
- **Review**

Review 3

☒ I read my piece to myself.

☐ My writing makes sense. **I think so**

☒ My name and the date are on my writing.

☒ I have a title for my writing.

☒ I used periods, question marks, and exclamation marks.

☒ I used capital letters.

☒ My final work is neat.

☒ This is my best work.

Figure 4.40 **Review 3 example**

Worksheet
The Super3: Review 4

- **Objective/Purpose:** Students will record 3 steps they completed to finish their task.
- **Context for Use:** For use when students have completed a task or assignment as a reflection on the process of their work.
- **Outcome:** Students will evaluate process of their work.
- **Tips:** It is helpful complete a few examples as a whole class first to outline teacher expectations.

IDEAS FOR TEACHING AND LEARNING

This is an exercise that will help children to sequence the steps they engaged in as they completed an assignment. Students should be encouraged to think about what they did and see if it matched the task requirements.

This can also be used as a whole class sequencing activity. As a group, the class can record what they did on a field trip, how they completed a group activity, or what they did in the morning or afternoon on a given day.

Super3
- **Plan**
- **Do**
- **Review**

Name:______________________________

Review 4

First I ______________________________

______________________________.

Next I ______________________________

______________________________.

Then I ______________________________

______________________________.

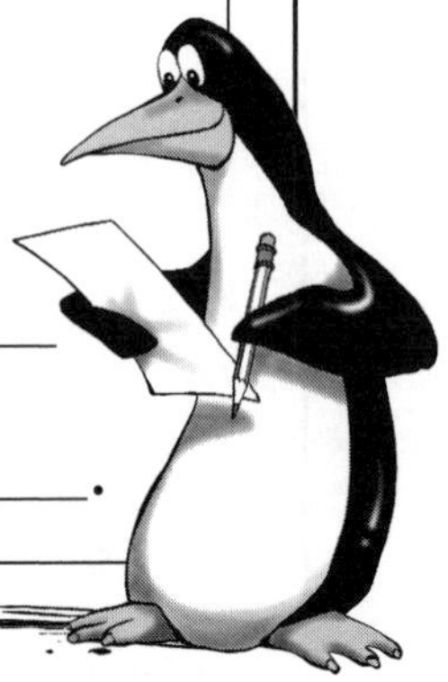

Figure 4.41 **Review 4**

Review 4

First I picked my animal from the list.

Next I used my book to learn about frogs.

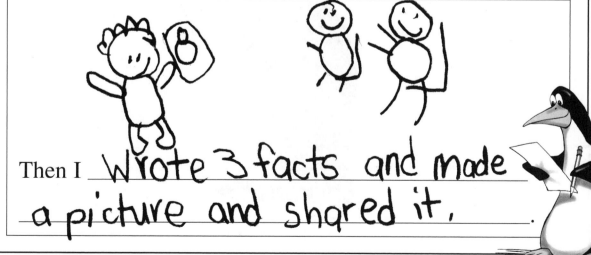

Then I wrote 3 facts and made a picture and shared it.

Figure 4.42 **Review 4 example**

Worksheet

The Super3: Review 4

- **Objective/Purpose:** Students will complete a self reflection on their overall learning about a specific topic or concept.
- **Context for Use:** For use after a specific topic or concept has been taught.
- **Outcome:** Students will evaluate their learning, understanding, and next steps for a particular topic or concept.
- **Tips:** This is great to use when determining if students comprehend and understand the material being taught.

IDEAS FOR TEACHING AND LEARNING

This activity helps students to look deeper into their work. It is a good worksheet to use after studying a certain topic or theme: plants, animals, life cycles, community helpers, or addition and subtraction math families. It is also interesting to do this as a whole class activity.

Super3
- Plan
- Do
- Review

Name: ____________________________

Review 5

I learned ____________________________

____

____

____________________________.

• • • •

I wonder ____________________________

____

____

____________________________.

• • • •

I still need to work on ____________________________

____

____

____________________________.

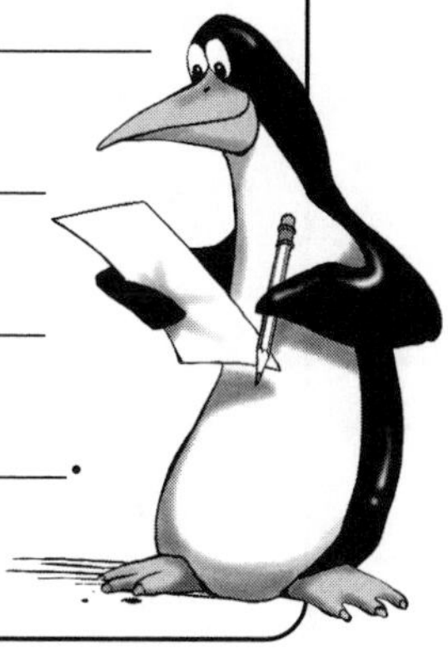

Figure 4.43 **Review 5**

Name:_____

Review 5

I learned _what stars are, how far away they are, what they are made up of._____ .

. . . .

I wonder _how scientists study about stars._____ .

. . . .

I still need to work on _____
_learning the constellations_____ .

Figure 4.44 **Review 5 example**

Chapter **5**

ADDITONAL IDEAS AND CONCLUSION

SOME FINAL THOUGHTS ABOUT THE WORKSHEETS

The Super3 worksheets provided in the previous chapter are designed for teachers to easily integrate into their daily activities and implement them within existing subject area curriculum, tasks, and assignments. The ideas we include are starting points, and we know (and hope) that teachers will individualize, customize, and add their own creative twists to best make them work for the given setting.

The worksheets offer specific tools, techniques, and strategies for immediate implementation of Super3 instruction. And, most importantly, the worksheets assist teachers to help young students become better thinkers and problem-solvers by learning and focusing on process.

Here's a final tip for using the worksheets: don't try to do too much at one time or with one worksheet. Make the worksheet work for you and the members of your class. We find it most valuable to break it down by each part of the Super3. Therefore, we made a special effort to keep the worksheets simple and focused on developing one skill or understanding. The worksheets help to design activities that will:

- Allow children to examine their task before they get started.
- Think about how they will complete the activity.
- Reflect on the final result of the task.

ADDITIONAL IDEAS

It's easy and fun to help students learn the Super3. This section provides a range of additional lessons and activities that we or others have used.

Lesson Idea 1: Developing a "Plan"

Even young children can understand the concept of having a plan. In focusing on the BEGINNING: Plan, we like to have students make choices and then put things together in a plan of their own. One of our favorite activities, is to give the students a 2x2 (two-by-two) choice chart.

For example, suppose the students' task is to make some form of a picture. They have to decide from choices they have to make that picture. We like to offer two typical choices:

    1. to color or draw.
    2. to cut out pictures and paste.

So, the students can choose either:

| Color or Draw | Cut and Paste |

Then, there's the choice of sources for students to use to gain the information for their picture. For almost all subjects of pictures, students have two major choices in terms of information sources:

    1. to talk with a person.
    2. to use a book or similar resource (print or electronic).

So, again, students can choose either:

| Person |
| Resource |

When putting it all together, each student has 1 of 4 possibilities in terms of plans:

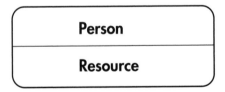

| Color or Draw/Person | Cut and Paste/Person |
| Color or Draw/Resource | Cut and Paste/Resource |

The result is a very quick, 2x2 plan!

There are lots of variations for this exercise. For example, the students can discuss the difference between coloring, drawing, cutting, and pasting. On the sources side, they can brainstorm different sources: people (teacher, parent, friend); resources (books, computer, magazines). Teachers can also give them other options to choose from. The main point is to get across the idea of thinking ahead and having a plan!

Lesson Idea 2: Brainstorming

Brainstorming with students is easy and fun. One of our favorite, on-the-spot activities is to pose an information problem to solve (for example, I need to buy a new toy for my baby), and have students brainstorm potential sources of information to help make this decision. Then, work with the students to decide which source is the "best" to check, and why. The students will want to talk about the actual toy, but the learning part is to have them realize that the information source is equally important as the final decision.

Lesson Idea 3: Citing Sources

Recording and citing sources is usually a new concept for young learners but one that ends up being an critical task for later years. Simple ideas for helping students to easily record their sources include:

- using a rubber stamp of a book, person, or computer to show where they found the information.
- having the student draw a picture of the source(s) they used.
- giving students stickers of appropriate sources (books, people, computer) that they must include on assignments.

Lesson Idea 4: Getting and Giving Feedback

It is often difficult for teachers to give accurate and appropriate feedback to all students for every assignment. Similarly, it can be challenging for students to provide their teacher with comments about particular tasks and assignments. One technique that we have tried to alleviate this communication concern is to have a "tape recording" station in the classroom or library for students to record information about their work (what went well, what would they do differently next time, or the easiest and hardest part of completing an assignment). In contrast, teachers can record personal comments for individual students to listen to. It is helpful to have guiding questions at the tape-recording station for students to think about before they record their thoughts. Another strategy is for students to first write their ideas down and then use their notes for the recording session. This set-up may take practice and time to get started but has proved to be extremely rewarding for students and teachers alike.

Lesson Idea 5: Bad Examples

To help students become more proficient with Review, show them a variety of completed assignment examples (these can be teacher created or samples from previous years) ranging from superior to horrible. Young learners often get a kick out of informally evaluating other work and seeing work that is incorrect, incomplete, or missing things. It is also interesting to try having students create a "good example" and a "bad example" and then discuss exactly what makes it "good" or "bad."

THE SUPER3 AND THE BIG6

As noted in the beginning of this book, the Super3 is intended for the very young. It is closely related to our popular and widely used Big6 approach. While many educators and parents have successfully used the Big6 with very young children, we felt that even six stages were too many to remember. So, we developed the Super3.

The Big6 is an approach that can be used whenever people are faced with an information problem or with making a decision that is based on information. Students—K-12 through higher education—encounter many information problems related to course assignments. However, the Big6 is just as applicable to their personal life.

The Big6 Skills comprise a unified set of information and technology skills (see Figure 5.1, page 95). Taken together, these skills form a process. The process encompasses six stages from Task Definition to Evaluation. Through the Big6, people learn how to recognize their information needs and how to progress through a series of stages to solve information problems effectively and efficiently. Many problem-solving models provide a set of specific activities, or outline of isolated skills. These models may encourage a lockstep strategy that forces one specific method for problem-solving and decision-making. Like these others, the Big6 approach is systematic, however, it differs in a significant way. Big6 Skills provide a broad-based, logical skill set that can be used as the structure for developing a curriculum or the framework for a set of distinct problem-solving skills. These fundamental skills provide students with a comprehensive set of powerful skills to conquer the information age.

But the Big6 is more than simple a set of skills—it is also an approach to helping students learn the information problem-solving process. Learning more about the Big6 as a process and as an approach should make it easier and more useful for teachers and their students. For teachers, the Big6 provides a definitive set of skills that students must master in order to be successful in any learning context. Teachers can integrate lessons about the Big6 into subject area content and assignments. For students, the Big6 provides a guide to dealing with assignments and tasks as well as a model to fall back on when they are stuck. The Big6 represents "metacognition"—an awareness by students of their mental states and processes.

FIGURE 5.1: **THE BIG6**

1. Task Definition:

    1.1 Define the problem.

    1.2 Identify the information needed.

2. Information Seeking Strategies:

    2.1 Determine all possible sources.

    2.2 Select the best sources.

3. Location and Access:

    3.1 Locate sources.

    3.2 Find information within sources.

4. Use of Information:

    4.1 Engage (e.g., read, hear, view).

    4.2 Extract relevant information.

5. Synthesis:

    5.1 Organize information from multiple sources.

    5.2 Present information.

6. Evaluation:

    6.1 Judge the result (effectiveness).

    6.2 Judge the process (efficiency).

Figure 5.1 **The Big6**

From experience and research, we found that successful information problem-solving does require completing each stage at some point in time: defining the task; selecting, locating, and using appropriate information sources; pulling the information together; and deciding that the task is in fact completed. However, the Big6 is not linear and prescriptive. It is not necessary to complete the stages in order, however all the stages must be completed at some time for overall success.

Over the years, we developed some key understandings about the Big6. These are highly relevant to the Super3 as well.

(1) The Super3 (and Big6) process can be applied in all subjects and across grade levels.

The Super3 and Big6 have been used with students and teachers in all subject areas and in all grade levels. In school, students must complete assignments and solve problems in every class, in every subject, and in every grade. Each time, to be successful, the students need to figure out what they must do, and then gather and work with some information to finally produce something (even if it's a short answer on a quiz), and make sure it's okay before turning it in. That's what the Super3 and Big6 are all about.

(2) The Super3 (and Big6) are adaptable and flexible; they can be applied to any information situation.

One of the major differences between the Super3 and Big6 Skills approaches and other information skills models are their broad applicability. In addition to school projects, reports, research papers, and assignments, the Super3 and Big6 are also applicable to everyday information problems, needs, and situations. Examples include deciding what TV show to watch or selecting a birthday present to buy someone. Talking through a personal decision-making situation can be fun, enlightening, and helps students learn the process.

(3) The Super3 (and Big6) are a "process" curriculum for integrating information literacy instruction with all subject area curricula at various grade levels.

The skills that are required to successfully solve information problems in science are the same skills needed in social studies, literacy, mathematics, art, or any of the other content areas. All students have information problems to solve, whether it is in a kindergarten lesson about community helpers, a 7th grade unit which requires students to compare igneous, metamorphic, and sedimentary rocks, or a 12th grade lesson on different forms of government throughout the world. We continually emphasize that teaching information skills is most effective when combined with current subject area units, lessons, and assignments.

(4) The Super3 (and Big6) reflect critical thinking as an information problem-solving process.

Inherent to the Super3 and Big6 approaches are their concerns with students' cognitive development. Thinking and reasoning skills are important skills that are central to the Big6 and Super3. By focusing on process, the Super3 and Big6:

- help students learn to ask good questions.
- teach students to independently organize and assess information.
- provide students with a strategy to logically and systematically solve information problems and evaluate solutions.

The Super3 – Big6 connection is a direct one, and there is an easy transition from the Super3 to the Big6.

Starting with the Super3, in the BEGINNING, children Plan. From a Big6 perspective, this means that children go through (1) TASK DEFINITION and developing (2) INFORMATION SEEKING STRATEGIES. Students are thinking about what they have to accomplish and the information they need to do it.

According to the Super3, in the MIDDLE, children Do. For the Big6, this means that students go through (3) LOCATION & ACCESS, (4) USE of INFORMATION, and (5) SYNTHESIS. There's a great deal for students to accomplish here—and both models provide ample explanation on how to go about it.

Lastly, at the END of the Super3 process, children Review what they have done to determine how well they did and how they might do better. The Big6 refers to this as (6) EVALUATION, and students assess the product (effectiveness) as well as process (efficiency).

Here is a matching exercise for students when they make the transition:

1 **Task Definition**

2 **Information Seeking Strategies**

Plan

3 **Location and Access**

4 **Use of Information**

Do

5 **Synthesis**

6 **Evaluation**

Review

Figure 5.2 **Big6 Super3 Matching**

THE SUPER3 IS FUN!

Most importantly, the Super3 should be FUN!!! Be creative and make learning the Super3 a beneficial and valuable experience for all. It should be easy for teachers and students alike to implement the Super3 into their daily routines and learning assignments.

SUPER3 BOOKMARKS AND POSTERS

There are a number of different Super3 bookmarks and posters available for classroom use….. or make your own! Hang the posters around your room (and even better, your school), give the bookmarks to students as individual or class rewards. Have a class contest to design a Super3 poster or create a class Super3 mascot, similar to our penguin. It is surprising how much children absorb when the content they are learning is around them in different formats.

Guidelines for use for making posters and bookmarks include: for education use only, they are not to be sold in any way, they should include the Super3 copyright.

SUPER3 DINOS

In Green Bay, Wisconsin, some creative teachers came up with the Super3 Dinos:

PLANasaurus

DOasaurus

REVIEWasaurus

Figure 5.3 **Super3 Dinos**

SUPER3 SONG

We've heard of raps, songs, and stories. Here's the song from our website:

Sung to the tune of "Bingo"

Words by Diana Cazares, Susan Hensley, and Karen Jordan, students at the University of Texas Graduate School of Library and Information Science, Austin, TX.

Here is a process I can use,
Its name is Super3-0!

Plan, do, and review;
Plan, do, and review;
Plan, do, and review;
Its name is Super3-0!

First I plan what I will do,
And look for what I need-o.

Plan, do, and review;
Plan, do, and review;
Plan, do, and review;
Its name is Super3-0!

Next I use what I have found,
And show what I have learned-o.

Plan, do, and review;
Plan, do, and review;
Plan, do, and review;
Its name is Super3-0!

Finally I review my work
And make sure it's my best-o.

Plan, do, and review;
Plan, do, and review;
Plan, do, and review;
Its name is Super3-0!

SUPER3 COLORING PAGES

Lastly, we offer these new Super3 coloring pages. We have some additional coloring pages on our website, but here is Super3 Sam!

Figure 5.4 **Penguin**

Plan

Figure 5.5 **Plan**

Do

Figure 5.6 **Do**

Review

As always, we are interested in hearing from you! How is the Super3 used in your classroom? What special and unique Super3 activities have you created? Share your ideas and read about other's!

There are several avenues and opportunities to touch base with us including:

- Big6 and Super3 website (www.big6.com)
- Big6 Listserv
- Big6 and Super3 eNewsletter

Thanks for reading! We sincerely hope implementing these activities proves to be SUPER for you and your kids!

— Mike and Laura

Index